For some, poetry arrives unannounced. It is very much like a hiccup. When it arrives it's very difficult to do much of anything else.

Kevin, my husband, as well as many of our friends, have come to realize that upon arrival, it is best to step aside and allow the poem to be written.

Afterwards, Kevin quietly reads, shakes his head, and gives me a smile. It has become a catch phrase between us for any moment that arrives without notice or effort, or as a gift... Kevin simply states, "It's like a poem...".

I call these moments... God.

Holy Hiccup An Interactive Journal of Poetry

Holy Hiccups

An Interactive Journal of Poetry

By Denise McCormick Baich

Holy Hiccups

This is a self published book by Denise McCormick Baich via Mira Digital Publishing.

Text Copyright © 2011 by Denise McCormick Baich

Cover photography by Hannah Hicks

All rights reserved under International and Pan-American Copyright Conventions. Published in the United States by Denise McCormick Baich via Mira Digital Publishing.

Dedication

I thank God, and my family and all my friends for this amazing experience. I pray that it will be enjoyed by many. I have been blessed with a wonderful and patient husband, my Kevin, and three exceptional and extremely talented and supportive girls, Lindsey, Kimberly, and Kelsey. Thank you for loving me, inspiring me, supporting me, and encouraging a quirk of mine that at times has no earthly explanation.

To my friend, Nate Voelker and his family, Cassie, Randal and Emma. Thank you for accepting me as I am, and challenging me during times I thought I had reached my limits. I find God and wondrous new potential awaiting - everytime.

To Chris Shank, who continues to help me understand and interpret the hiccups that arrive to this day. No matter how difficult or challenging the words are that must be written down, I am free to record it without fear of judgment, and then seek Chris's awesome input.

To Wendy Sain and Kelly Vincent for welcoming this odd and flighty gift and novice poet and helping me embrace God's gift and find joy in the most unsuspected moments... your encouragement is always truly priceless.

To Michael McIntyre. I have grown from sitting in the back of the room and feeling lost, shallow, and unworthy when I walk into church, to sitting _almost_ in the front row in Celebration Hall, and this is no small feat. I now desire a loving and blessed relationship with Our Lord and Savior and I am constantly learning how strongly God feels the same. I have so far to go, but I treasure how God speaks through you.

Holy Hiccups are met with a thirst, which is why a glass of water was perfect for the cover of this book, thank you Hannah Hicks. In so many ways, thirst applies to us all. In Ghana, to quench a thirst is to give new hope, new life. In our own communities here in the United States, to quench people's thirst for Our Lord and Savior is very much the same. I feel poetry is God's gift given to help quench my undying thirst and the feeling is something that I wish everyone could experience. With this being the first collection of Hiccups put into publication, my family and I know that it would not have been possible without the support of our church family, Living Word.

Ten percent of the proceeds from this gift will be given to Living Word to help with whatever the call, whether it is in Ghana or in our communities here at home... God willing, we pray that this gift will enable us to do so much more!

Holy Hiccup An Interactive Journal of Poetry

Prologue

A Holy Hiccup

That repeated convulsion.
The body and mind's involuntary, uncontrollable attempt…
To right itself.

When something so basic…
Must be corrected.
And it occurs without our prior knowledge or consent.

But regardless of our attempts to stop it,
The spasms continue.
Until once again all is well.

The Holy Hiccup…
Upon it's unannounced arrival it brings with it a light-hearted recognition.
Attempts to function while inflicted may draw giggles from all.

Over time a questioning sets in…
As moving about our regular business becomes difficult,
Almost hindering whatever task we take on.

As these unpredictable heaves continue…
A discomfort can develop into actual pain,
Forcing His recognition and address to the forefront.

But Ahhhhh… after the battle…
The rest when the struggle is done.
A hiccup… A Holy Hiccup… Enjoy!

Denise McCormick Baich

Holy Hiccup An Interactive Journal of Poetry

If Only to Ask the Caterpillar

If only to ask the caterpillar,
What secrets could it possibly know,
When deciding it's time to build it's cocoon...
And within this shelter to go.

Are there pains during it's transformation?
Is there a moment it can change it's mind?
Are there thoughts of how it wishes to change...
Of what color? What shape? And what kind?

Or could such a tiny insect,
Truly display what some wise men don't know.
That only with *FAITH* in Our Lord's intentions...
Will our real beauty blossom and grow.

Denise McCormick Baich

Holy Hiccup An Interactive Journal of Poetry

"It Truly Is What It Is!"

When it seems all is different around you,
And even the familiar takes on a new view,
It is time to grab hold of the ole mirror,
And turn it directly pointed at you.

It doesn't mean that things are not positive,
It certainly doesn't mean there is something wrong.
It just means that life has taken a turn,
And it may be something that's been coming all along!

The time has come for you to now decide,
Are these changes welcome or something to dread?
Is the world around you actually different,
Or are these changes strictly just in your head?

If the things around you are left to morph,
And become what they will inevitably be,
Will the results be a world that will wonderfully exist,
And contribute to what you wish to see?

No change comes without discomfort.
A few treasures will be left along the way.
Some events and friendships once held dear,
Become blessed memories with each passing day.

But with a clear understanding of what God's goal is,
And how your final days would wish to unfold,
Any change that occurs daily around you,
Can be as precious and vibrant as gold!

When we know change is a part of God's plan,
And each occurrence is ultimately His.
The reflection we will see can be celebrated…
And we can sing, "It truly is what it is!"

Denise McCormick Baich

Holy Hiccup An Interactive Journal of Poetry

The Heart or the Mind?

The heart or the mind?
Which one lends to our behavior?
Our heart or our mind?
Which one *should* we favor?

To be able to think,
And resolve the world's woes.
Yes, the mind is important,
Shouldn't do without it, I suppose.

But, Ahhhhh! The wondrous heart!
A moment without it and there's no mind.
A fleeting… moment… without it…
No thoughts will we find.

If one's heart is truly healthy,
And by that I mean much more than just beating.
If this heart is kind and gentle and good
And it's focus on Heaven leading.

Is it not the heart?
To which we imply?
When we "Go with our gut"…
And seem to get it just right?

Our heart is like the beacon,
For which our mind can reach.
It's vision toward the future…
With God's goals shining for each.

And as we listen closely to our heart…
And make sure that we do what is best,
The light of each beat will spread 'round the world,
To Bless and be seen by the rest!

So please ponder your thoughts intently,
But don't disregard feelings of any kind,
For it is truly your precious HEART…
Which is supporting your human mind.

Denise McCormick Baich

Holy Hiccup An Interactive Journal of Poetry

"YES"

The Poetry Society Membership,
Was a gift from my husband on my 46th Birthday.
For years he would patiently read and listen...
To what my poetic scribbles would convey.

For years the words would strangely arrive,
As emotional thoughts undaunted.
The poems would come and weigh on my heart...
(A writing utensil was all I wanted!)

So many poems have come and gone,
For years I thought unworthy to save.
Out with the trash, gone with life's passing...
(Lord only knows to whom that I gave!)

I gathered the few poems within arms reach,
To take to the first poet's reading,
I decided to hold off on my religious works...
To avoid offending on what society deems "leading".

As I arrived and took my seat,
I strategically offered to read after some...
So as to hear the poets that came before,
I would then decide which poem was the one.

I heard many beautiful writings,
So diverse in their story and prose.
With only one mentioning of our Lord,
Then within me a message arose...

"Yes" (cont'd)

I was avoiding reading my poetry...
That mentioned God or any passage of the same,
I then heard "I have given you this opportunity,
So then why do you not mention My Name?"

So suddenly my turn was upon me,
The poem so obvious that needed to be read.
It was as if I spoke from within my heart...
Each precious phrase that needed to be said.

I watched each facial expression...
As each word slowly fell to the floor.
Would the words of our Lord be rejected?
Or would they in fact want to hear more?

The veteran sitting to my right...
Who read before me with piss and vinegar,
Leaned toward me while furrowing his brow,
But visibly appeared much kinder and gentler.

A woman sitting to my left...
Suddenly cracked a subtle smile,
And clasped her hands together...
Nodding slightly all the while.

"Yes" (cont'd)

A photographer slowly lowered her lens,
As if suddenly taken by surprise,
Then quickly regained her composure...
With clear acceptance in her eyes.

As I finished the poem of my choice...
And raised my head to view the crowd,
The silence was almost deafening...
The quiet approval extremely loud.

"Would you like to hear another?"
(The answer would be anyone's guess)
A loving whisper touched my soul...
I heard them answer... "Yes"

Denise McCormick Baich

Perfection

The perfection of imperfection.
How beautiful it truly can be.
The tarnished green patina of copper.
The aged character of a crooked tree!

With perfection we know what is expected,
And we can anticipate what we might see.
But within the unpredictability of imperfection,
Is where we will find hope and God's majesty.

Denise McCormick Baich

Holy Hiccup An Interactive Journal of Poetry

Reflections

What a wondrous invention,
The mirror has turned out to be!
Saving us from moments of embarrassment…
Smiling with fresh food between our teeth.

It seems so readily available,
As it hangs waiting on our wall.
It let's us know when our clothes are a mess,
Or if our hair is threatening to fall!

But quite often this dependable item,
Is not as friendly or cordial as most.
How we wish it could give us adulations!
"You look wonderful!" We wish it could boast.

During these moments of wondering and primping,
I ponder what our real desire might be…
Is it actually finding our *INNER* beauty?
And not just what others might see?

Denise McCormick Baich

Holy Hiccup An Interactive Journal of Poetry

Within Your Grasp

There are moments when some feel so alone,
When in truth our God is there.
And recently I came to a little revelation,
That I really would like to share…

At birth we are simply unshaped clay,
It is our surroundings that create what we become.
A few have influence readily within their grasp…
And quite a challenge is posed for some.

When my children were tiny and learning to crawl,
I would sit at a near distance and gently call their name.
They knew I was there, they would roll they would stretch…
And then one day on their little knees… they came.

And as they grew it was time to walk,
I would stay in sight but just a few steps away.
They would teeter, they would falter, and occasionally bounce,
But within arms reach they knew I would stay.

When I hovered and did not require them to try,
No effort did my little ones make.
Until the moments I required them to move on their own,
That's when the first wobbly steps they did take.

As we grow it is His challenge…
Of reaching and achieving our goal.
That molds and makes us what we are,
It's in the foundation of our very soul.

So in the moments you feel you are alone,
Please know that God is ready to share.
He is waiting just within your grasp,
Just reach… and God is there.

Denise McCormick Baich

Poetry Reading

Sitting in a room full of poets.
Beauty resting, much like a garden of flowers just waiting to bloom.
A few faded and drooping… spent early, with a desire to be fed.
Many are vibrant and budding, reaching for their true potential…
Guided by a limit set only by the Glorious Son.
Rooted solidly in fertile poetic soil.
All… Soaking up the atmosphere thick with creation.
Drinking in the sound…
Breathing out the words.

Denise McCormick Baich

Holy Hiccup An Interactive Journal of Poetry

Holy Hiccup An Interactive Journal of Poetry

Masterpiece

Words are my paint,
So I close my eyes and load the tray.
The pen is my brush.
Paper is now my canvas.
The subject for my artwork,
Is our Lord and Savior, Jesus Christ.
I liberally lift the color of peace,
And gently spread it across the smooth linen.
I dab delicately in forgiveness,
And feather it amongst the peace…
Blending… slowly…together…
Something is needed…
Ahhhh!
The color of Faith.
This becomes the background – the foundation,
Beautifully encompassing Our Lord.
I touch the crimson color of pain,
And rest my brush sorrowfully upon His body…
His head, His back, His feet, His hands – His heart.
It is time to add His brilliance!
This color was so very easy to find!
It shown as if it chose me!
I make sure to include shading,
For without the dark…
We can't fully yearn for His light.
I step back and draw a breath…
And I discover…
Our Lord and Savior is the Artist…
And WE are His Masterpiece.

Denise McCormick Baich

This poem was inspired by a call for Artwork from Tim Bastron

Holy Hiccup An Interactive Journal of Poetry

Marinate

I have noticed that many thoughts,
Are now a lot like fast food.
It's so quick and easy…
To just drive through.

What has happened to pondering?
Taking in a thought… and then plan it's preparation?
To pound it, to flip it around, drop it in a dish…
And marinate it.

Then after a timely soak.
Place it on the grill… sear it,
Turn it, press it… flatten it out.
Allow it to rest once again.

Then sit back and taste it.
Gingerly cut it up, chew it slowly…
Savor the tenderness and flavor,
And then…. beautifully present these thoughts.

Serve them…
On fine transparent china.
In portions easily governed by our guests,
And on a table set for all who wish to dine…

On thoughts allowed to marinate.

Denise McCormick Baich

Holy Hiccup An Interactive Journal of Poetry

Church Coffee Pots & Parking Lots

In the past I have seen the frustration,
As people drove into a church parking lot.
I also could see small signs of hurried angst,
As they waited at the church coffee pot.

A parking lot is ever present.
Like Heaven; welcoming and so easy to find.
Readily available for all who wish to enter.
Easy to maneuver for those with an open mind.

Yet sometimes a parking lot can pose a challenge.
For some just looking for that "perfect" spot.
Quite often they arrive and travel in circles,
Cause what they "wanted" just isn't where they thought.

Around the coffee pot it can be warm and inviting,
But when we are sleepy and not quite aware,
We may forget others in need are also in line,
And with patience there will be plenty to share.

A cup of coffee can be invigorating,
Much like our faith and God's community.
I now understand why we truly desire,
To fill our cups with His Faith, Hope, and Charity.

So the next time I am in the church parking lot,
I will let the rushed stranger have my spot.
I then will look forward to "resting" in line,
With all my friends at Our Lord's coffee pot.

Denise McCormick Baich

*A poem inspired by a Chris Shank Challenge.

God's Mystery

The Sanity of insanity.
The Calm of calamity.
The Incompleteness of finality.
The Restoration of rest.

The Hope of the truly hopeless.
The Perfection of imperfection.
The Direction of misdirection.
The Burden of the blessed.

The Goal without expectation.
The Humbleness of glory.
The Grace of the downtrodden.
The True Faults within our best.

The Life that only comes from dying.
The Rise that will only occur after the fall.
The Alpha and the Omega.
God's Mystery is there for us all.

Denise McCormick Baich

God Knows That You So "CAN"

God *KNOWS* that you so "*CAN*"…
He has tremendous faith in you.
He already knows that you are very capable,
But do *YOU* know what *YOU* can do?

Much like the request of Peter,
When he called to Jesus from within a boat.
As Jesus stood upon the water...
Peter asked to also be kept afloat.

As Peter suddenly panicked and began to sink,
"Oh, man of little faith" Our Jesus did say.
Our Lord had every confidence in Peter,
… Then Peter began to pray…

With trust in Jesus you can stay afloat,
But give fully with faith in all you do.
Because Our Lord *KNOWS* that you are capable,
It is time to have faith…in His Faith… in *YOU*.

Denise McCormick Baich

Holy Hiccup An Interactive Journal of Poetry

A Choir is Like a Piano

A choir is like a piano,
Each key with its own lovely sound,
But when combined to play one gentle tune,
Emotions long forgotten are found.

A hug can reach one person,
As wonderful as that may be,
But a choir lifting song can touch more hearts
Than our eyes can possibly see.

Denise McCormick Baich

Holy Hiccup An Interactive Journal of Poetry

Forgiveness is His Key

I do believe forgiveness is the key,
From the prison in which we are entrapped.
Unwittingly burying ourselves deeper,
When anger is the cloak in which we are wrapped.

In fact Our Lord gave us His Key…
He willingly turned it over.
And showed us how with forgiveness,
We can release ourselves - the true prisoner.

If Jesus could lovingly look into the eyes,
Of the individual driving the nail…
I know that we can learn to fully forgive,
And with His Key we can truly prevail.

Denise McCormick Baich

I Am His Pen

I find poetry throughout my day,
In every word I hear and say.
In the quivering tone of a baby's cry.
In the gentle hiss of it's mother's sigh.

To close my eyes and take the time,
To just breath in each soothing rhyme.
And wish upon my friends and foes,
To also experience God's wonderful prose.

To listen to the wind and find,
A beautiful sound of a different kind.
Of love lifted high upon an angel's wing,
It is His forgiveness for which they sing.

Even in moments of deep despair,
I also find His poetry there.
His promise that there is no end,
And, He, in fact, is a waiting friend.

I find poetry throughout the day,
In every sound which passes my way.
And I know each tone and delicate song,
Conveys God's love; faithful and strong.

I listen and breath in each sound He's conveyed.
I site each verse and hum each tune played.
For God is the poet and I am His pen,
And I will write down His poetry again, and again…

Denise McCormick Baich

Holy Hiccups An Interactive Journal of Poetry

"Self-ish"

Are we so bold to believe it IS what we know?
That our "perfection" is what God would wish?
Or possibly that "imperfect" day was exactly what we needed,
For us to find our "kind" and become a lot less "self-ish."

Denise McCormick Baich

Holy Hiccup An Interactive Journal of Poetry

His Quilt

On this beautiful Sunday morning,
We willingly come and gather in His place.
A Quilt of many distant tattered souls,
Of varied origin… color… and face.

The Quilt of God's Church is infinite,
And opens wide to welcome us in!
There is no limit to who can become a part…
Not country… Not gender… Not skin.

The thread of our voice is tremendously strong!
Woven together to honor His name.
The rainbow of dialects intertwined,
Combine together to be a part of the same.

The pattern for this Quilt was long ago cast,
By Our God, Our Jesus, Our Lord.
He knew the Creation that would encompass us all,
And the price paid He would knowingly afford.

The Maker of this glorious Holy Creation,
Never tires of what He must do…
But with each scrap that He is beckoned to bring within,
God lovingly mends us and makes us anew.

Denise McCormick Baich

*This poem was inspired by a Nate Voelker request.

Holy Hiccup An Interactive Journal of Poetry

Death's Door

Why is it we dread this passageway?
Why is it we avoid it at all costs?
Why is it a door that we desperately struggle to avoid?
Why do we call it's occupants "lost"?

Why do some anticipate it's presence,
With such doom and undefined dread?
Why do the residents of this earthly existence,
Call the blessed entrant's of this door "dead"?

Can't we see the welcome mat awaiting?
Can't we see the wreath upon this door?
Adorned with broken thorns and God's forgiveness…
With the most beautiful branches… and more!

Can't we see how wonderful this door is to enter?
Just how amazing the other side will be?
In God's time this glorious entrance will welcome us all,
It is our task to just find His Key…

Denise McCormick Baich

Holy Hiccups An Interactive Journal of Poetry

Breathe

Breathe…
Don't speak
Breathe…
And just listen

Breathe…
Wiggle your toes
Breathe…
Inhale just through your nose.

Breathe…
Relax those shoulders
Breathe…
And let peace take over

Breathe…
Close your eyes
Breathe…
And release a few sighs

Breathe…
Think of our Lord
Breathe…
Think of His grace.

Breathe...
Feel His Love.
Breathe…
Envision His face.

Breathe…
And release all fear.
Just Breathe…
For we know He is near.

Denise McCormick Baich

"Be still and know that I am God!" Psalm 46:10

This one... is for my Dad.

Holy Hiccup An Interactive Journal of Poetry

"Feelin' Alittle Crazy"

Why do I feel half "crazy"…
When God does exactly what He told my heart He would do?
With each promise He has made plainly obvious,
God's love for me is becoming increasingly true.

So there are moments I want to turn to my neighbor,
And declare… "Hey! Did you see that?!"
"God and I had this awesome conversation…
And He *said* He would take care of that…"

But I find myself cautiously taking pause,
And just putting this declaration aside…
This is just a secret between God and me,
A little something to just keep inside.

Wait!…

That is NOT what God and my heart wants to do!
I wish to talk about it throughout my day.
Everyone should want to experience This love…
It's all I want to do, sing and say!

So, SURE! I'm feelin' a little "crazy"…
And with my friends and neighbors I'll share,
His awesome, amazing, tremendous love,
And the FACT that I know He is there.

Denise McCormick Baich

Holy Hiccup An Interactive Journal of Poetry

The Mighty Kumquat

So what is a kumquat?
An orange-like fruit with an edible sweet rind.
And when you get to the pulp…
It's of a sweet and tart meaty kind.

Don't be fooled by it's nature,
Though smaller than it's distant orange brother,
The flavor this small fruit packs within,
Can't be matched by any other.

Growing high upon a flowering tree,
Taking it's time to ripen to it's season.
The respect and admiration it has acquired,
Truly stands up to anyone's reason.

Much like a Christian grows into their own,
It takes time to become what we ought…
But through faith and patience in what God has created,
Life can be as sweet as the Mighty Kumquat.

Denise McCormick Baich

* A Poem inspired by a Nate Voelker Challenge

Holy Hiccup An Interactive Journal of Poetry

As I Sit in Silence…

As I sit in silence,
And long for His grace,
I feel the fear down to my core,
The wet tears upon my face.

Oh, God, how could such things occur?!
Such innocence be lost…
How could such evil walk the earth,
And at such a staggering cost?!

As I can't help but hit my knees,
And cry out in audible pain…
I recognize these trials and disasters,
Awaken us to God's power again.

Why should we have to be brought to this point?
It should be so easy to see…
That only through His peace and forgiveness,
How beautiful this world can be!

Denise McCormick Baich

Holy Hiccup An Interactive Journal of Poetry

To Cherish This Very Moment

To cherish this very moment,
Is to pay homage to every passed day.
To extend our respect to each precious word,
Our friends and family would say.

To cherish this very moment,
We appreciate what's justly and unjustly sowed.
The mothers, the daughters, our babies and Grandmas,
Our childless, our divorced, and our widowed.

To cherish this very moment,
Is to celebrate the life changes shown.
The weddings, the births, and the successes with work…
ALL God's blessings known and unknown.

To cherish this very moment,
Means to open our hearts like a book.
To gently inscribe each fleeting occurrence,
Every hug. Every scent. Every look.

To cherish this very moment,
We must see just how fragile life is.
How today we will dance, and tomorrow we'll rest,
And when God calls some will no longer exist.

To cherish this very moment,
Is to know that our time is a gift.
Each tick of the clock a beautifully wrapped trinket,
To embrace. To treasure. And to lift.

To cherish this very moment,
Is to give it away without concern.
To willingly provide our hearts and our minds,
To love. To console. And to learn.

So please cherish this very moment.
Draw close to those here to share.
It is but one Our Lord has created…
To laugh. To cry. And to care.

Denise McCormick Baich
*A poem inspired by a Jackie McCormick request for the Living Word Women's Banquet.

Holy Hiccup An Interactive Journal of Poetry

Christianity is My Home…

Christianity is my precious home,
With many rooms, windows, and doors.
Furniture for beloved guests,
With soft carpeting and hard floors.

There are rooms that welcome many,
And rooms which are my very own.
There are rooms meant just for clutter,
And rooms where treasures are shown.

There are rooms with lighting a plenty!
And rooms where the illumination is low.
There are rooms of which I am not proud,
And rooms I feather for show.

This structure changes with the seasons,
And requires my constant care.
I diligently give it the attention it needs,
So I know it will fully be there.

As the winds blow and the rains do fall,
I will sit peacefully within this home and rest.
And when the Son arrives and knocks on my door,
He can see I have tried my best.

It truly is an endless task,
To lovingly maintain this wonderful place.
Christianity is my refuge,
It is my God-given space.

Denise McCormick Baich

Holy Hiccup An Interactive Journal of Poetry

...And His Footprint Grows Again!

I have discovered that with relationships,
People we care for must come and go.
I have found we are all part of Our Lord's foot print,
With ten precious and wonderful toes.

Now initially they all appear separate,
But when we carefully look deeper in,
The toes are intricately bound together,
By His beautiful bones and His skin.

As we come together to honor God's word,
This mark increases in it's size.
Each footprint that is left behind...
Plainly grows before our very eyes.

So although we may not be in the same place,
We must know we are bound together by His skin.
Our love for Christ leaving His mark,

...And His footprint grows again!

Denise McCormick Baich

Holy Hiccup An Interactive Journal of Poetry

Where Do We Find The Answer?

Where do we find The Answer?
On Facebook, within texts, or on twitter?
Life holds so many challenges and rewards,
Ranging from bliss to extremely bitter.

So many wandering aimlessly,
Believing the answers can be found on a screen.
When actually real peace and tranquility,
Is quite often silent and unseen.

The momentary comment,
Easily accessed with a password and ID.
Replacing The Answer easily found,
When just looking inside of "ME".

No batteries are needed.
No outlet has to be used.
No volume switch, no access code.
No "ratings" of how it amused.

The Answer is with us always.
In our hearts God's great love does abound..
Just ask and He shall be given.
Just seek and He shall be found.

Denise McCormick Baich

Holy Hiccup An Interactive Journal of Poetry

Same Ole, Same Ole…

I wish it was obvious to see,
Exactly what it is He wants from me…
It seems that I simply pray and pray,
But it's all the same at the end of my day.

I search my soul for His inspiration,
So I can actually change the situation…
To what God might want life to be,
But the same ole, same ole is all I see.

Bring on His Hope… and bring it now… Amen.

Denise McCormick Baich

*This was written "on empty" and just before an awesome experience.
I hope it can also be a gift to others.*

Holy Hiccup An Interactive Journal of Poetry

Without a Second Thought

To look at the world and hurt for it's faults,
And know that my child is it's cure.
To willingly give of His life for their sakes,
Is something I know I could not endure.

Why could it be so challenging for some,
To feel the sheer vastness of His love?
To believe that this love is only limited,
To the angels and puffy clouds from up above?

Our Lord sent His son without a second thought,
To live… and to die… for our sins.
To just open our hearts and accept this sweet gift,
And that is where Heaven truly begins.

Denise McCormick Baich

Life's Carousel

There are moments we watch life's carousel…
Adorned with so much beauty and sound.
It becomes so easy to lose track of time,
As we stare at it turn round and round.

We realize it could be our turn to step aboard,
And choose which beast will be our steed.
So many choices are readily within our grasp,
Yet not one appears to take the lead.

It would be so simple to stay on this ride,
To mount up and join in the race!
But suddenly we discover this fantastic machine,
Truly begins and ends in one place.

The real challenge is presented when we must step down,
And courageously exit this spinning ride.
Never again to travel in enchanting circles,
And contently walk away… with God at our side.

Denise McCormick Baich

Where Something Familiar Meets the Unknown

As I happily escape the constraints of my shoes,
My toes feel the breeze and venture willingly into the familiar sand.
The sound of water upon water churning loudly in my ears...
And I admire the clash of two worlds meeting, the water and the land.

A walk from the sharp sand dried under the harsh exposure of sun,
Onto a smooth surface where water has gently let it's presence be known.
My footprints momentarily leave a mark... then are washed away,
Blending with a surface on which I am now but a memory... forgiven.

The beach seems to be a place to which many are drawn.
A place where something familiar meets the unknown.
We are able to approach it, dip our toes in it... submerge in it.
Of our own choice, we can venture as deep as our courage will allow.

As the elements of cool soothing water and foam roll over my feet,
The desire to walk farther in is strong.
The fear of what lurks beyond my sight,
Briefly holds me from feeling the sweet relief waiting further in.

I draw a breath and travel deeper,
And feel the embrace of wonderful texture and current...
Pulling me... begging to engulf all my senses,
Welcoming me to become a part of it's power.

As the new strength of each wave arrives I am drawn in...
My fears are released with each anticipated ebb and flow,
And an insurmountable desire arrives to become a part...
I clasp my hands together and dive in.

Denise McCormick Baich

His Star

As I rested in silence,
At the end of my day.
I opened my Bible,
And read what Matthew had to say.

In this chapter it tells,
Of three Kings and His star.
And I yearned for such a brilliant sign,
To show us exactly where You are.

As I glanced out the window,
Into a beautiful dark night.
A part of me knows there is struggle,
Just beyond my blurry sight.

They too are searching for Our Savior's star,
Even if they don't truly yet know.
What is it that we all must say…
And where is it that we must go?

Then a wonderful peace gently arrived,
And it seemed to radiate from my core.
A new awareness of where my search begins,
So much clearer than before.

So many long years have passed now,
Since the Kings had to travel afar.
The Answers for us can be found in His Book,
And within our hearts we can carry His star.

Denise McCormick Baich

Holy Hiccup An Interactive Journal of Poetry

The Rhyme and Reason Deep Within

Poetry resides deep within us.
It is found in a place that is so raw and uncharted,
That it's low and gentle recitation can physically move even the heaviest of souls…

The guttural purging of a poem,
Can exhaust even the strongest of individual,
And reduce them to tears of jubilation or sorrow with only a phrase, a word…
a glance…

Simply being in a poem's proximity,
Has the potential of leaving a mark so profound,
That the desire to revisit it's contents will live on forever.

An addiction sowed simply by it's reading,
Instills within the user their need to go back over and over and over…
To permanently tattoo the words on a reader's consciousness so as to feed their need.

The healing of Poetry so profound,
That as the nurturing words flow across mind and tongue,
One can watch as the sufferer morphs into a state of serenity…

The intertwining of reason and rhyme, contradiction and contemplation…
Something about it lends to Poetry's unleashed power,
Which causes the poem to reside deep within us...

….It is found in a place that is so raw and uncharted…
That it's low and gentle recitation can physically move even the heaviest of souls…

Denise McCormick Baich

Speechless

At times there are no words.
To say what needs to be said…
So how does one communicate…
When speechless

When a moment reaches this point,
It has truly escalated beyond earthly bonds.
And beckons for validation…
When speechless

When belief is beyond verbal expression,
No longer discerned by a worldly definition.
Only to be confirmed by emotion, touch and sight…
When speechless

A blessing, a miracle, an answer to a prayer…
To which there can be only one explanation.
That is where we find God…
When speechless

Denise McCormick Baich

In The Shadow of the Jet Stream

We are living life at sonic speed!
It seems the day ends before it begins.
Running to work, caring for the kids,
And, of course, so are our friends.

It seems no matter the effort we make,
There is *always* another need.
So we pick up the pace… step on the gas,
And continue at sonic speed.

Society tells us how we should continue our lives,
With *this* gadget or paying *that* cost.
But while traveling so fast to keep up this pace,
How many of God's joys have we sadly lost?

How I wish we could **STOP**….
                Just simply rest…
                    In a field…
                          Much like a dream…
Resting peacefully within God's joy…
Content in the shadow of the jet stream.

Denise McCormick Baich

*This poem was inspired by a Nate Voelker Challenge.

Epiphany

To ache down to the core,
For injustice that makes no fathomable sense.
And realize what has to be done,
Will occur at your own expense.

But for love and a true existence,
It is a price you are willing to pay.
In the hopes that peace and tranquility,
Will be a reality for all some day.

What an epiphany Our Lord must have come to,
When He wept and grieved for us all.
That He in fact would truly suffer,
And on the cross His blood must fall.

Denise McCormick Baich

The Perfect Day

From a disconnected distance it was just an exchange,
From those who-have to those who-have-not.
But for those who wish to remain at this distance...
Take a seat and listen closely you ought.

It was a sunny day with distant clouds,
With wonderful gifts and volunteers abounding.
All was set in place and prepared for the day,
With food, fun, and great music sounding.

The forecast said rain and that was okay,
It brought breezes and cool temperatures needed.
The guests did arrive with smiles on their faces
Gently par-taking of what was "unspokenly" needed.

Then suddenly the breeze became a gust,
And did lift the tent where many stood.
The next turn of events defined the event,
And truly molded this day... as it should.

At the moment the tone went from festive to fear,
And the wind caused the children to shudder.
The people transformed from haves and have-nots,
To concerned friends, family, sisters and brothers.

As the thunder did roll and lightening arrived,
We ALL rushed to the Church for protection...What a Perfect
Day and awesome turn of events!
When we look back on it in loving reflection.

Denise McCormick Baich

Her Backpack

An assignment completed,
A lunch packed and ready to go,
Some shoes for Phys Ed,
And spelling words she'll need to know.

A permission slip that Dad signed,
A library book that needs read,
A braided friendship bracelet,
And a note with what the teacher said.

She carries within this backpack
More than just items or random things.
For within this very backpack
She is prepared for what her day brings.

For some it's not so simple…
Their day begins with much less.
From where will they fill this backpack…
And with what is anyone's guess.

To provide this simple blessing,
Can give hope where once there was none...
To FILL this little satchel,
Is to share God's Hope with a little one.

Denise McCormick Baich

Holy Hiccup An Interactive Journal of Poetry

Imago Dei

God made man like his Maker.
Like God did God make man.
Each person in His Image,
Each creation a part His plan.

To come to this realization,
Is to know it is not just our skin.
It is the discovery and actualization,
Of true love that comes from within.

This is not limited by time or distance,
Or by language and frame of thought.
This is a deep down realization...
Of His truth and what He has taught.

God's gift of bearing His image,
Speaks beyond any border or wall.
It is not limited by gender or color,
His likeness is encompassing of all.

So as we enter a place of strangers...
Please know it is God that you see.
For we are all created in His image,
Alleluia! Imago Dei!

Denise McCormick Baich

This poem was inspired by a Nate Voelker request.

Lent and the Man from Nantucket

There once was a man from Nantucket,
Who had only foul words in his verbal bucket,
But with the onset of Lent and his forgiveness not spent...
I know Heaven is still waiting once he chucks it.

Denise McCormick Baich

*Another poetic challenge from Nate.

Holy Hiccup An Interactive Journal of Poetry

Holy Hiccup: An Interactive Journal of Poetry

"More Than Just A Storm…."

As the storm clouds gathered,
I began to mentally prepare.
Would it be a direct hit?
Or quickly turn gentle and fair?

Would the winds churn the branches,
While the air turns thick with wet?
Would the drops come soft and caressing,
Or unjustly angry, swift… and violent?

Should I stand and face the window?
Should I welcome the fate it would bring?
Should I move to shelter and wait…
Buried, secure …. and cowering?

As indecision lends to my pause,
I light a candle should the lights go out.
Giggling with the trivial effort,
Compared to the storms potential clout.

The sirens distant moan,
Impress upon my indecision,
The danger quickly closing in,
Just beyond my line of vision…

I herd my family downward,
To the safety of the basement.
Delicately calming our dog Bonnie,
Visibly shaking with the torment.

"More Than Just A Storm...." (cont'd)

As we huddle in the confines,
Of a cedar closet assembled just for storage.
I look for much needed supplies...
Should the worst require us to forage.

As the minutes pass like hours,
And every rumble becomes a roar...
I pray for family, I pray for friends...
I think of yesterday and the day before...

Could this storm bring more than weather?
Has it brought reflection only accessible through fear?
Does it carry with it the power of awareness,
When we must gather in a moment what's dear?

Then I realized the very instant,
I closed that basement door,
This storm wasn't just bad weather,
It in fact was so much more.

The thought that came upon me,
As I gathered what truly meant most,
Is the love I have for my family and friends...
And my Faith in Our Heavenly Host.

Denise McCormick Baich

*This poem arrived after the Joplin, Missouri tornado of 2011.

Holy Hiccup An Interactive Journal of Poetry

The Grand Total

Life is much like counting...
Some tally fast and some will count slower.
Some will diligently site every digit,
And some get the chance to start over.
Eventually we all will reach our total,
And for each it just isn't known...
But everyday we must keep on counting...
Until the day His grand total is shown.

Denise McCormick Baich

The Register

T'is a beautiful season,
When we pause to take in the sites.
With snow and garland and tinsel galore,
With bows and soft twinkling lights!

Was there a register present on that precious day?
Were there short commercial breaks?
Can't we see the diversions from His Holy Birth,
That taking on too much of these practices makes?

Tradition is good and I see it's worth,
In sharing and giving with much care…
But do we remember the Reason for the Season,
And why Jesus in the manger was there?

Denise McCormick Baich

Holy Hiccup An Interactive Journal of Poetry

Seek

If you close your eyes...
Do my words still exist?
If I write them in simple terms,
Will your mind give them a twist?

Our truth is not meant to be clear as crystal.
God's Truth is for us to continuously seek...
Do we grow stronger when we exert no effort?
Or does that leave us empty and weak?

Denise McCormick Baich

Holy Hiccups An Interactive Journal of Poetry

If I Have A Good Life…?

If I have a good life…
Should I feel terribly bad?
Does it mean I should be aching so inside,
And give away all that I have?

For what is it I strive for?
If not peace and a place to rest my head?
Three square meals, a happy family,
With loving words always said?

If I have achieved this …..
Should I feel undeserving and unjustly blessed?
Have I unwittingly hung myself out to dry,
By succeeding and doing my best?

If I give and give until it hurts,
So that my family must now struggle,
Does it not mean I have added to the chaos?
Aren't we then lending to the trouble?

It would seem that those not truly in need,
Yet continue to lean upon those who are able to give,
Are the ones that we should appeal to at this time,
To help us focus on those truly just trying live.

It has become so EASY…
For some to just sit and receive.
When actually they are capable,
But now simply wish to deceive.

How can we come together?
Those who have and those who have not,
And see the world that God intended,
And actually give harmony a real shot.

If I Have A Good Life…? *(cont'd)*

If I have a good life…
Yet others don't strive for their own…
How can my giving till it's all gone,
Bring God to whom He's not known?

I am not blessed with this wisdom.
I have fear and infinite concern.
Please answer me this question…
And with God's help maybe I'll learn.

Denise McCormick Baich

"I Am Here"

So I had this dream…
And within it a door.
I stood safely on one side,
The other… no floor.

I heard her approaching,
And watched as she fell.
No matter my effort,
She chose to fall in this well.

I cried out in terror.
I screamed out in fear.
It seemed no one was listening,
And no one could hear.

She was not responding.
At the bottom she remained.
I pulled and I shouted,
I reached and I strained.

Then during a moment,
Of sadness and grief,
A voice arose from the well,
To my disbelief.

He said, "Do not worry",
He said, "Do not fear",
"Your Loved One will be ok…."
He said, "I am here."

Denise McCormick Baich

Gray Hair and Grace

For others it most certainly may be different,
But for me it happened slowly and at the same time.
I had recently started to discover our Lord,
And stopped using hair color to save a dime.

Initially I didn't appear much different.
My daily routine was much the same.
But then slowly others started noticing,
Some liked it, and others?... I won't mention their name...

Now when making these changes it's a progression,
But it seems that one day you suddenly wake up,
And truly your someone different,
Regardless of your clothes and the makeup.

With Gray hair and Grace it is similar.
It is subtle but then shines like the Son.
The trick is learning to embrace it,
Then allow yourself to just be... and go have some fun!

Denise McCormick Baich

The Power of a Tear

The power of a tear...
Have we had it all wrong?
The strength of a crying person,
Thought to be weak for so long?

After all of these years...
The person silent and unmoved.
Truly the very needy one,
Recent events have now proved.

What fortitude we have seen,
In the trust openly shown,
By the soft weeping sufferer,
Letting their feelings be known.

The reason for the hurt...
Placed on open display,
Allowing into their hearts,
The loving words people say.

Crying is weak?
Silence is strong?
Could it honestly be true...
That we've had it so wrong?

Nations travel afar,
And strangers draw others near,
To comfort and console...
The shear power of a tear.

Denise McCormick Baich

Holy Hiccup An Interactive Journal of Poetry

Hope Can Be Found In All Places

Hope can be found in all places.
In different colors shapes and kinds.
The sources for hope are only limited,
By the boundaries of our hearts and our minds.

For one it is a distant siren,
As they wait below fallen debris.
For another it is a high hilltop,
As they run from the surging sea.

For the new mother swollen and aching,
It is a picture with ten fingers and toes,
For the debtor who thought there was no relief,
It is the money he can give to who's owed.

For a child it is a backpack,
Filled to the brim with the supplies they might need.
For an unemployed mother and father,
It is a meal and family they can now feed.

It is the smile you gave the teller,
As she struggled with her long day.
It is the kind word shared with the waitress,
Holding the door, sharing a hug, or that gentle wave.

Hope comes from seeing through God's perspective.
He inspires each action our heart makes.
God can change what seems unchangeable,
In the midst of crisis God's Hope is all it takes.

Hope can be found in all places,
And today we find Him fully within you!
Each soothing note and precious chord,
Shine in all you sing, say, and do!

It is the Great Awakening!
To know that God's Hope is what one can give.
Each action you take, each kindness you make,
May be the HOPE another needs to just LIVE.

Denise McCormick Baich

*This poem was inspired by a Nate Voelker request.

The Shore

*A boat
Is each life
Every moment,
The current.*

*Our will
Is the oar.
Our goal...
Heaven... the Shore.*

Denise McCormick Baich

"Please Answer…"

Tap… tap…. tap…. Gently on my consciousness.
What could that possibly be?
A forgotten item, event… a memory?
I dismiss the inquiry and continue about my tasks.
Tap, tap, TAP… once again.
I gently wipe my brow and breath a sigh…
Everything around me appears just as it was.
Bystanders seem unaware… or are they?
Tap, TAP, TAP… On my heart…
Ouch! Can't others feel this too?!
My breath quickens and tears fill my head…
Warm ice cubes now reside in my throat.
I fight back the surge of water and emotion…
My Irish nose turns bright red under the strain.
TAP, tap… knock, Knock…
I have no choice but to stop, stunned… motionless.
"Truly!!" I beckon … drawing a breath, and tightly
closing my eyes.
Knock, knock, KNOCK…
My soul cries out, "OH, My Goodness! Oh, My Lord!"…

"Yes… Please answer…"

Denise McCormick Baich

Holy Hiccup An Interactive Journal of Poetry

Holy Hiccup An Interactive Journal of Poetry

Flighty Poet

I acknowledge I am a flighty poet,
And what I see is not what others may see.
The ramblings sounding quite silly,
The career path not what others may wish to be.

The thought of putting into writing,
All emotions or thoughts that come to mind,
May strike others as kind of awkward,
And not quite of the "normal" kind.

To see things just on the surface.
To limit imperfection as something to shun.
To behave as others would wish me,
Will not be how my life is done.

To be a flighty poet,
Means to fly freely above the norm…
To see the simplest of God's beauty,
In every shape, sound, and form.

So, yes, I have moments of awkward,
But for those who accept what I will be,
Know that they just have to pick up my poems…
And they can fly just as high as me!

Denise McCormick Baich

Holy Hiccup An Interactive Journal of Poetry